~A BINGO BOOK~

Native Americans Bingo Book

COMPLETE BINGO GAME IN A BOOK

Written By Rebecca Stark

Educational Books 'n' Bingo

ISBN 978-0-87386-454-1

Educational Books 'n' Bingo

Printed in the U.S.A.

NATIVE AMERICANS BINGO DIRECTIONS

INCLUDED:

List of Terms

Templates for Additional Terms and Clues

2 Clues per Term

30 Unique Bingo Cards

Markers

1. **Either cut apart the book or make copies of ALL the sheets. You might want to make an extra copy of the clue sheets to use for introduction and review. Keep the sheets in an envelope for easy reuse.**

2. Cut apart the call cards with terms and clues.

3. Pass out one bingo card per student. There are enough for a class of 30.

4. Pass out markers. You may cut apart the markers included in this book or use any other small items of your choice.

5. Decide whether or not you will require the entire card to be filled. Requiring the entire card to be filled provides a better review. However, if you have a short time to fill, you may prefer to have them do the just the border or some other format. Tell the class before you begin what is required.

6. There are 50 terms. Read the list before you begin. If there are any terms that have not been covered in class, you may want to read to the students the term and clues before you begin.

7. There is a blank space in the middle of each card. You can instruct the students to use it as a free space or you can write in answers to cover terms not included. Of course, in this case you would create your own clues. (Templates provided.)

8. Shuffle the cards and place them in a pile. Two or three clues are provided for each term. If you plan to play the game with the same group more than once, you might want to choose a different clue for each game. If not, you may choose to use more than one clue.

9. Be sure to keep the cards you have used for the present game in a separate pile. When a student calls, "Bingo," he or she will have to verify that the correct answers are on his or her card AND that the markers were placed in response to the proper questions. Pull out the cards that are on the student's card keeping them in the order they were used in the game. Read each clue as it was given and ask the student to identify the correct answer from his or her card.

10. If the student has the correct answers on the card AND has shown that they were marked in response to the *correct questions,* then that student is the winner and the game is over. If the student does not have the correct answers on the card OR he or she marked the answers in response to *the wrong questions,* then the game continues until there is a proper winner.

11. If you want to play again, reshuffle the cards and begin again.

Have fun!

TERMS

Algonquin (Algonkin)

Apache

breechclout

buffalo

Cherokee

Chief Joseph

Chilkat

clan(s)

coup(s)

cradleboard(s)

Creek(s)

Five Civilized Tribes

Great Basin

Haida

horse

Indian Territory

Iroquois

Iroquois Confederacy

kachinas

lacrosse

maize

medicine bundle

moccasins

Navajo

Northwest Coast

Osceola

parfleche

pemmican

plank house(s)

Plains

Pomo

porcupine quills

potlatch(es)

Pueblos

Sacajawea

Sequoyah

Seminoles

shield

sign language

Sioux

Squanto

Tecumseh

tepee (tipi)

totem pole(s)

Trail of Tears

travois

vision quest

wampum

wigwams

winter counts

Additional Terms

Choose as many Native Americans terms as you would like and write them in the squares. Repeat each as desired. Cut out the squares and randomly distribute them to the class. Instruct the students to place the square on the center space of their card.

Native Americans Bingo

Clues for Additional Terms

Write three clues for each of your Native Americans ters.

 1. 2. 3.	 1. 2. 3.
 1. 2. 3.	 1. 2. 3.
 1. 2. 3.	 1. 2. 3.

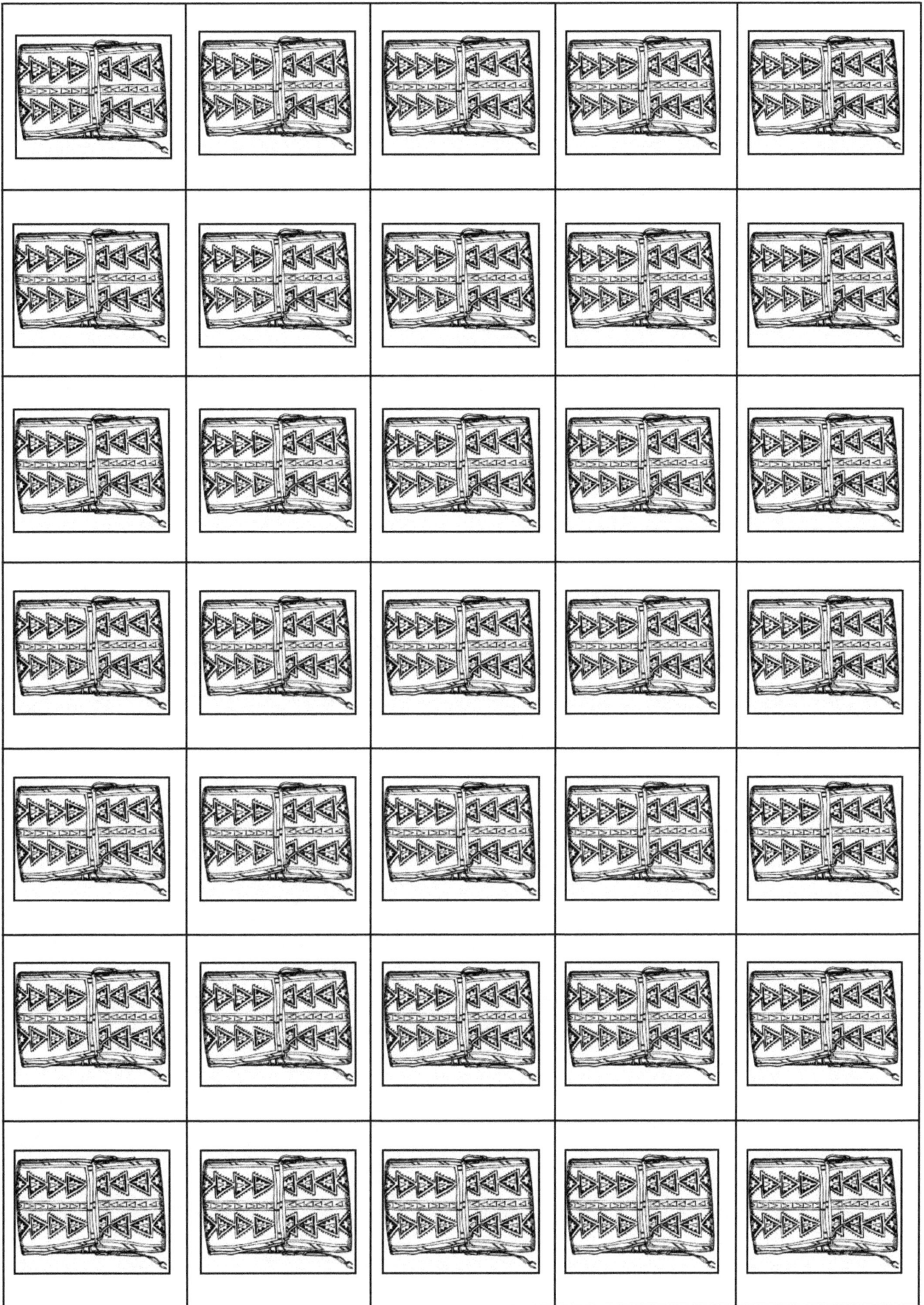

Algonquin (Algonkin) 1. Along with the Iroquois, these tribes inhabited the Northeast Woodlands. Some ___ tribes include the Mohegans and the Mohicans. 2. The concept of *manitou* was an important part of ___ religion.	**Apache** 1. Along with the Navajo and the Pueblo, the ___ lived in the Southwest and parts of the Great Plains. They often raided their neighboring tribes. 2. These people of the Southwest were fierce warriors. Geronimo was an ___.
breechclout 1. It is a long, rectangular piece of tanned deerskin, cloth, or fur. Most Native American men wore some form of it. 2. Men wore it between their legs and tucked over a belt. It left their legs bare, so many men also wore leggings.	**buffalo** 1. The Plains Indians depended on this animal for food, clothing, and shelter. 2. Hunting ___ became easier for the Plains Indians when they got the horse.
Cherokee 1.They were one of the so-called Five Civilized Tribes and published books and newspapers in their own language. 2. Sequoyah was one. He invented a ___ syllabary.	**Chief Joseph** 1. He was a Nez Percé chief. 2. He is known for his surrender speech in which he said, "My heart is sick and sad. From where the sun now stands I will fight no more forever."
Chilkat 1. The___ were a northern tribe of the Tlingit and were known for their exquisite blankets. 2. ___ blankets were highly prized. They were made of mountain goat wool and cedar-bark string.	**clan(s)** 1. It is a kinship group. 2. The Haida belonged to one of two ___: the raven ___ or the eagle ___.
coup(s) 1. On the Plains warriors sometimes earned points for touching an enemy. It was called counting ___. 2. A warrior's status was based on his bravery. To count ___ a warrior used either his ___ stick or his bare hand.	**Cradleboard(s)** 1. This baby carrier allowed the mother to work and the baby to feel safe and secure. 2. Most ___ allowed the baby to move only his or her head.

Creek(s)

1. The Muskogee were an important tribe in the ___ Confederacy.

2. The ___ were one of the Five Civilized Tribes. There were more than 50 towns in the ___ Confederacy.

Five Civilized Tribes

1. These tribes were called this because they adopted many of the whites' ways and had fairly good relations with them.

2. The so-called ___ included the Cherokee, the Chickasaw, the Choctaw, Creek and Seminole.

Great Basin

1. Conditions were harsh for the Paiute and other tribes of the ___.

2, The Paiute and others of the ___ fished and hunted. They supplemented their diets by gathering pine nuts and berries.

Haida

1. These people of the Pacific Northwest built large plank houses

2. These people of the Pacific Northwest were known for their skillfully crafted canoes made from red cedar trunks.

horse

1. When the ___ was introduced to the Plains, the hunting of buffalo became more efficient.

2. With the introduction of the ___ by the Spanish, many sedentary tribes became nomadic.

Indian Territory

1. This was land set aside for Native Americans in an area that is now Oklahoma.

2. Many Native Americans were forced to go there as a result of the Indian Removal Act of 1830.

Iroquois

1. These people of the Northeast lived in multi-family homes called longhouses.

2. Unlike the Algonquins who also lived in the Northeast, life for the ___ centered around farming.

Iroquois Confederacy

1. The Mohawk, Seneca, Cayuga, Onondaga, and Oneida were members of the ___. (Later the Tuscarora joined.)

2. The Mohawk were called "Keepers of the Eastern Door" by other members of the ___.

kachinas

1. In Pueblo religion they are the spirits of their ancestors who visit.

2. Masked dancers impersonate ___ during Pueblo agricultural ceremonies.

lacrosse

1. The game of ___ was invented by Native Americans. It was played by many tribes and was sometimes played to resolve conflicts.

2. ___ games were sometimes major events that lasted for days.

Native Americans Bingo

maize	medicine bundle
1. Also known as corn, it is the most widely grown crop in the Americas. 2. In many traditions of the Northeast Woodlands ___ was one of the "three sisters." The other 2 were beans and squash.	1. Some Native American men carried a ___ with a collection of items of spiritual value to them. 2. Items put in a ___ might include animal teeth or claws, seeds, or anything else of spiritual meaning to the owner.
moccasins	**Navajo**
1. Most Native Americans wore this type of footwear. 2. In the Northeast ___ were soft soled. On the Plains the ___ had hard, rawhide soles.	1. Their homes were called hogans. 2. They held elaborate healing ceremonies involving sand paintings.
Northwest Coast	**Osceola**
1. Forests along the ___ provided cedar for the people's homes and canoes. The waters provided salmon and food. 2. Among the tribes of the ___ were the Haida, the Nootka, the Tlingit and the Tsimshian.	1. He was a Seminole chief. 2. He led a small band of resistance during the Second Seminole War. He was tricked into surrendering.
parfleche	**pemmican**
1. It is a rawhide container used by the Plains Indians. It was often used to carry pemmican. 2. These rawhide containers were often painted with geographical features.	1. This food mixtures was made of dried meat, fat and sometimes fruit. 2. The Plains Indians carried ___ in their parfleche as an emergency food supply.
plank house(s)	**Plains**
1. Many tribes of the Northwest Coast lived in ____. 2. The___ of the Haida and other Northwest tribes were made from thick cedar boards lashed to a wooden frame.	1. The buffalo provided for almost all of the needs for many Native American tribes of the ___. 2. The horse was very important to the buffalo hunters of the ___, such as the Comanche, Arapaho and Cheyenne.

Pomo

1. The baskets made by the ___ of California are considered by many to be the best in the world.

2. The ___ used coiling, twining and other techniques to make their exquisite baskets.

porcupine quills

1. Many Native American tribes decorated their clothing, baskets and other objects with ___.

2. Embroidery with ___ became less important when glass beads became available through trade with Europeans.

potlatch(es)

1. Status was based upon wealth along the Northwest Coast. Guests were invited to ___ to receive food and gifts.

2. Along the Northwest Coast ___ were held to celebrate important occasions, such as the birth of a child.

Pueblos

1. The ___ lived in the desert areas of the Southwest in multi-story houses made of adobe and stone.

2. The ___ village was built around the kiva, which was used by the men for ceremonial or council meetings.

Sacajawea

1. She was the Shoshone woman who accompanied the Lewis and Clark Expedition.

2. She acted as interpreter for Lewis and Clark on their expedition.

Sequoyah

1. He invented the Cherokee syllabary, sometimes called the Cherokee alphabet.

2. His invention of the syllabary led to the creation of the first Native American newspaper, *The Cherokee Phoenix.*

Seminoles

1. Many ___ hid in the Everglades of South Florida to avoid removal to Indian Territory.

2. Their huts are called chickees. They were made of palmetto thatch over a cypress-log frame.

shield

1. This piece of equipment was very important to the Plains warrior. It was painted with symbols representing the warrior's spiritual life.

2. The ___ of a Plains Indian provided spiritual as well as physical protection.

sign language

1. Native Americans used ___ for intertribal communication.

2. Children were taught ___ at a very early age so they could communicate with people from other tribes.

Sioux

1. Sitting Bull was a ___ leader in the Battle of Little Bighorn, where General Custer and his men were defeated and killed.

2. Crazy Horse was a fierce ___ warrior.

Squanto

1. He was a Patuxet Indian living in a Wampanoag Village when Samoset introduced him to the Pilgrims.

2. He helped the Pilgrims by teaching them how and when to plant corn and how and where to fish.

Tecumseh

1. He was a Shawnee warrior.

2. He sided with the British during the War of 1812 and was killed in battle.

tepee(s) (tipi)

1. The homes of the Plains Indians are called ___.

2. ___ were large conical tents made of animal skins over a framework of poles.

totem pole(s)

1. The Haida and other Pacific Northwest tribes constructed ___. Some were 40 feet high.

2. The symbols carved and painted on the ___ represented the owner's family and ancestry.

Trail of Tears

1. It refers to the forced relocation of the Indians to Indian Territory as a result of the Indian Removal Act.

2. The Cherokee gave this name to their trek from their homeland to Indian Territory, which is present-day Oklahoma.

travois

1. A ___ is a device for transporting belongings. It consists of 2 poles joined by a frame and is pulled by an animal.

2. When the horse __ replaced the dog ___, the Plains Indians could transport larger tepees.

vision quest

1. In some Plains tribes young men went on a ___ to acquire spiritual direction.

2. The ___ sometimes involved isolation and fasting.

wampum

1. These beads were sometimes used by the Iroquois to record agreements.

2. The most famous example is the Hiawatha Belt. It commemorated the League of the Great Peace of the 5 original Iroquois Nations,

wigwams

1. Most Algonquins lived in conical or dome-shaped ___; however, some lived in longhouses.

2. The Algonquins' ___ were made by covering wooden frames with birch bark.

winter counts

1. Many Plains tribes kept ___ to record the most important event of each year. (Some tribes recorded twice a year.)

2. ___ were made on buffalo hides. A new year began with the first snow.

Native Americans Bingo

Native Americans Bingo

Navajo	Maize	Totem Pole(s)	Wigwams	Travois
Coup(s)	Algonquin	Wampum	Porcupine Quills	Iroquois Confederacy
Sioux	Seminoles		Osceola	Potlatch(es)
Winter Counts	Apache	Kachinas	Tecumseh	Northwest Coast
Parfleche	Great Basin	Cradleboard(s)	Iroquois	Lacrosse

Native Americans Bingo

Winter Counts	Squanto	Plank House(s)	Sacajawea	Parfleche
Northwest Coast	Porcupine Quills	Breechclout	Apache	Sign Language
Sequoyah	Great Basin		Creek(s)	Kachinas
Horse	Tepee	Seminoles	Pemmican	Iroquois Confederacy
Lacrosse	Wampum	Cradleboard(s)	Coup(s)	Iroquois

Native Americans Bingo: Card No. 2

Native Americans Bingo

Winter Counts	Kachinas	Porcupine Quills	Tecumseh	Sioux
Great Basin	Algonquin	Chilkat	Maize	Moccasins
Apache	Wampum		Sign Language	Buffalo
Seminoles	Sequoyah	Parfleche	Horse	Plank House(s)
Iroquois	Coup(s)	Cradleboard(s)	Pemmican	Totem Pole(s)

Native Americans Bingo: Card No. 3

Native Americans Bingo

Seminoles	Sign Language	Parfleche	Coup(s)	Totem Pole(s)
Plains	Breechclout	Maize	Sacajawea	Sioux
Osceola	Horse		Travois	Wigwams
Kachinas	Shield	Wampum	Cradleboard(s)	Chilkat
Medicine Bundle	Lacrosse	Pomo	Iroquois	Potlatch(es)

Native Americans Bingo

Lacrosse	Travois	Apache	Breechclout	Coup(s)
Plains	Kachinas	Chilkat	Creek(s)	Algonquin
Squanto	Potlatch(es)		Five Civilized Tribes	Haida
Iroquois Confederacy	Sign Language	Navajo	Pemmican	Medicine Bundle
Porcupine Quills	Cradleboard(s)	Shield	Seminoles	Osceola

Native Americans Bingo

Buffalo	Sign Language	Plank House(s)	Squanto	Potlatch(es)
Tecumseh	Apache	Medicine Bundle	Maize	Sioux
Sacajawea	Chilkat		Breechclout	Creek(s)
Cradleboard(s)	Parfleche	Pemmican	Pomo	Osceola
Northwest Coast	Kachinas	Navajo	Totem Pole(s)	Shield

Native Americans Bingo: Card No. 6

Native Americans Bingo

Navajo	Sign Language	Haida	Five Civilized Tribes	Porcupine Quills
Northwest Coast	Totem Pole(s)	Great Basin	Algonquin	Plains
Plank House(s)	Wigwams		Creek(s)	Cherokee
Seminoles	Horse	Sioux	Winter Counts	Sequoyah
Cradleboard(s)	Coup(s)	Pemmican	Pomo	Buffalo

Native Americans Bingo: Card No. 7

Native Americans Bingo

Osceola	Sign Language	Clan(s)	Tecumseh	Cherokee
Plains	Squanto	Sacajawea	Potlatch(es)	Breechclout
Sioux	Pueblos		Totem Pole(s)	Travois
Iroquois	Seminoles	Winter Counts	Medicine Bundle	Horse
Wampum	Cradleboard(s)	Pomo	Apache	Northwest Coast

Native Americans Bingo

Creek(s)	Porcupine Quills	Great Basin	Sioux	Potlatch(es)
Medicine Bundle	Squanto	Osceola	Apache	Totem Pole(s)
Moccasins	Navajo		Algonquin	Clan(s)
Cherokee	Lacrosse	Parfleche	Five Civilized Tribes	Haida
Horse	Pemmican	Chilkat	Winter Counts	Travois

Native Americans Bingo

Winter Counts	Tecumseh	Breechclout	Sacajawea	Shield
Potlatch(es)	Cherokee	Maize	Algonquin	Totem Pole(s)
Pueblos	Sign Language		Wigwams	Sequoyah
Parfleche	Iroquois Confederacy	Medicine Bundle	Pemmican	Moccasins
Chief Joseph	Northwest Coast	Plank House(s)	Lacrosse	Osceola

Native Americans Bingo

Buffalo	Sign Language	Apache	Medicine Bundle	Northwest Coast
Clan(s)	Moccasins	Five Civilized Tribes	Creek(s)	Maize
Plains	Squanto		Plank House(s)	Great Basin
Chief Joseph	Sioux	Pemmican	Coup(s)	Winter Counts
Chilkat	Cradleboard(s)	Navajo	Pomo	Porcupine Quills

Native Americans Bingo

Porcupine Quills	Travois	Moccasins	Tecumseh	Creek(s)
Great Basin	Wampum	Squanto	Pomo	Algonquin
Navajo	Haida		Potlatch(es)	Sacajawea
Cradleboard(s)	Horse	Totem Pole(s)	Winter Counts	Plains
Sign Language	Clan(s)	Pueblos	Chilkat	Cherokee

Native Americans Bingo: Card No. 12

Native Americans Bingo

Chief Joseph	Travois	Buffalo	Moccasins	Potlatch(es)
Squanto	Clan(s)	Sign Language	Creek(s)	Sequoyah
Tecumseh	Breechclout		Great Basin	Haida
Osceola	Pemmican	Cherokee	Pueblos	Winter Counts
Cradleboard(s)	Iroquois Confederacy	Pomo	Navajo	Five Civilized Tribes

Native Americans Bingo

Coup(s)	Squanto	Apache	Pemmican	Chief Joseph
Cherokee	Navajo	Moccasins	Algonquin	Sign Language
Medicine Bundle	Wigwams		Plank House(s)	Chilkat
Iroquois Confederacy	Creek(s)	Pueblos	Breechclout	Buffalo
Cradleboard(s)	Sacajawea	Sequoyah	Northwest Coast	Osceola

Native Americans Bingo

Five Civilized Tribes	Creek(s)	Apache	Porcupine Quills	Tecumseh
Buffalo	Plank House(s)	Maize	Squanto	Medicine Bundle
Potlatch(es)	Navajo		Sioux	Totem Pole(s)
Cradleboard(s)	Moccasins	Clan(s)	Pemmican	Chief Joseph
Northwest Coast	Horse	Pomo	Shield	Great Basin

Native Americans Bingo

Breechclout	Moccasins	Clan(s)	Shield	Tepee
Sacajawea	Sequoyah	Haida	Plains	Wigwams
Chief Joseph	Travois		Potlatch(es)	Great Basin
Seminoles	Cherokee	Cradleboard(s)	Five Civilized Tribes	Winter Counts
Medicine Bundle	Vision Quest	Pomo	Horse	Sign Language

Native Americans Bingo

Chief Joseph	Trail of Tears	Indian Territory	Moccasins	Coup(s)
Five Civilized Tribes	Medicine Bundle	Pemmican	Wigwams	Haida
Creek(s)	Winter Counts		Vision Quest	Clan(s)
Lacrosse	Northwest Coast	Osceola	Apache	Sequoyah
Parfleche	Chilkat	Porcupine Quills	Tecumseh	Travois

Native Americans Bingo

Shield	Pueblos	Cherokee	Medicine Bundle	Sacajawea
Sign Language	Chief Joseph	Parfleche	Potlatch(es)	Chilkat
Creek(s)	Sequoyah		Indian Territory	Totem Pole(s)
Lacrosse	Maize	Pemmican	Winter Counts	Plank House(s)
Vision Quest	Moccasins	Apache	Trail of Tears	Buffalo

Native Americans Bingo

Potlatch(es)	Buffalo	Moccasins	Clan(s)	Pueblos
Five Civilized Tribes	Tecumseh	Totem Pole(s)	Porcupine Quills	Wigwams
Trail of Tears	Coup(s)		Algonquin	Shield
Plank House(s)	Vision Quest	Parfleche	Horse	Indian Territory
Sioux	Tepee	Northwest Coast	Osceola	Pomo

Native Americans Bingo

Pueblos	Trail of Tears	Tecumseh	Moccasins	Algonquin
Breechclout	Great Basin	Plains	Parfleche	Sacajawea
Travois	Haida		Seminoles	Maize
Lacrosse	Osceola	Iroquois	Horse	Vision Quest
Kachinas	Wampum	Tepee	Winter Counts	Indian Territory

Native Americans Bingo

Five Civilized Tribes	Buffalo	Plains	Moccasins	Iroquois Confederacy
Travois	Indian Territory	Cherokee	Clan(s)	Navajo
Sequoyah	Northwest Coast		Trail of Tears	Apache
Parfleche	Porcupine Quills	Vision Quest	Lacrosse	Osceola
Seminoles	Tepee	Pomo	Chief Joseph	Horse

Native Americans Bingo

Sioux	Plank House(s)	Indian Territory	Squanto	Chief Joseph
Sacajawea	Tecumseh	Shield	Clan(s)	Algonquin
Cherokee	Wigwams		Navajo	Haida
Vision Quest	Lacrosse	Horse	Maize	Coup(s)
Tepee	Chilkat	Trail of Tears	Sequoyah	Plains

Native Americans Bingo

Breechclout	Trail of Tears	Porcupine Quills	Squanto	Pomo
Buffalo	Pueblos	Northwest Coast	Five Civilized Tribes	Maize
Plank House(s)	Chief Joseph		Iroquois	Navajo
Sequoyah	Tepee	Vision Quest	Chilkat	Horse
Iroquois Confederacy	Osceola	Wampum	Parfleche	Indian Territory

Native Americans Bingo

Breechclout	Chief Joseph	Coup(s)	Trail of Tears	Clan(s)
Potlatch(es)	Pomo	Plains	Sacajawea	Navajo
Haida	Shield		Pueblos	Sequoyah
Iroquois Confederacy	Iroquois	Vision Quest	Chilkat	Travois
Kachinas	Seminoles	Tepee	Tecumseh	Wampum

Native Americans Bingo

Seminoles	Plains	Trail of Tears	Apache	Indian Territory
Maize	Iroquois Confederacy	Five Civilized Tribes	Breechclout	Algonquin
Travois	Clan(s)		Iroquois	Vision Quest
Shield	Lacrosse	Wampum	Tepee	Wigwams
Pomo	Coup(s)	Cherokee	Medicine Bundle	Kachinas

Native Americans Bingo: Card No. 25

Native Americans Bingo

Indian Territory	Trail of Tears	Iroquois	Sacajawea	Shield
Parfleche	Tecumseh	Clan(s)	Pueblos	Breechclout
Iroquois Confederacy	Plank House(s)		Wigwams	Seminoles
Chief Joseph	Squanto	Lacrosse	Tepee	Vision Quest
Haida	Medicine Bundle	Apache	Wampum	Kachinas

Native Americans Bingo

Iroquois	Cherokee	Trail of Tears	Pueblos	Great Basin
Iroquois Confederacy	Plank House(s)	Five Civilized Tribes	Vision Quest	Algonquin
Pemmican	Wampum		Tepee	Seminoles
Shield	Buffalo	Plains	Kachinas	Maize
Chief Joseph	Wigwams	Indian Territory	Sioux	Haida

Native Americans Bingo: Card No. 27

Native Americans Bingo

Potlatch(es)	Pueblos	Winter Counts	Trail of Tears	Cherokee
Great Basin	Indian Territory	Iroquois	Parfleche	Wigwams
Wampum	Sequoyah		Shield	Sacajawea
Haida	Sioux	Northwest Coast	Tepee	Vision Quest
Squanto	Creek(s)	Chief Joseph	Kachinas	Iroquois Confederacy

Native Americans Bingo

Indian Territory	Pueblos	Shield	Five Civilized Tribes	Creek(s)
Iroquois Confederacy	Parfleche	Plains	Haida	Sioux
Travois	Iroquois		Algonquin	Trail of Tears
Great Basin	Lacrosse	Totem Pole(s)	Tepee	Vision Quest
Breechclout	Clan(s)	Kachinas	Buffalo	Wampum

Native Americans Bingo

Coup(s)	Trail of Tears	Sacajawea	Creek(s)	Vision Quest
Maize	Totem Pole(s)	Plank House(s)	Wigwams	Algonquin
Kachinas	Chilkat		Haida	Plains
Iroquois Confederacy	Buffalo	Pueblos	Tepee	Iroquois
Lacrosse	Porcupine Quills	Wampum	Indian Territory	Shield

www.ingramcontent.com/pod-product-compliance
Lightning Source LLC
LaVergne TN
LVHW061338060426
835511LV00014B/1990